Forest

moor or less

Dawn Bauling
Ronnie Goodyer

Indigo Dreams Publishing

First Edition: Forest moor or less
First published in Great Britain in 2020 by:
Indigo Dreams Publishing
24, Forest Houses
Cookworthy Moor
Halwill
Beaworthy
Devon
EX21 5UU

www.indigodreams.co.uk

Dawn Bauling and Ronnie Goodyer have asserted their right under the Copyright, Designs and Patents Act 1988 to be identified as the authors of this work.
© 2020 Dawn Bauling & Ronnie Goodyer

ISBN 978-1-912876-27-3

British Library Cataloguing in Publication Data. A CIP record for this book can be obtained from the British Library.

Designed and typeset in Palatino Linotype by Indigo Dreams.
Cover design by Ronnie Goodyer
Printed and bound in Great Britain by 4edge Ltd.

Papers used by Indigo Dreams are recyclable products made from wood grown in sustainable forests following the guidance of the Forest Stewardship Council.

For those who have walked with us in the forest
and for those who have yet to tread there

FOREWORD

Life brought us together later than we would have liked, but it brought us to Cookworthy Forest at just the right time. It sits between the coast at Bude and the high moor of Dartmoor, 1,600 acres of managed Forestry England forest: conifers, oak and beech in beautiful harmony. It rests at the bottom of our garden like an ever-present counsellor and playmate; it has provided us with a place to wander in, to find consolation, to laugh and to listen. We have walked there with those closest to us, taken them by hand or in our heads. We have watched it, in all its essential, multi-coloured hues, letting it teach us things about ourselves, what matters, what doesn't, and giving us insight into the other places we have wandered in.

This joint collection is not just our response to that invitation, it is a thank you to those who have encouraged the pathways and journeyings, letting us find a rare and wonderful contentment.

Dawn and Ronnie

CONTENTS

Forest

moor or less

'Together we reach outwards and onwards,
each gleaming life intertwined
in the endless and eternal ceremony of being.'

~ *Path*, Louisa Thomsen Brits

Crescent Moon Over Cookworthy Forest

There is a new story in the Devon borderlands.
We are opening the pages together, learning as we go.
The words were written over the centuries
the book hidden for most of our lives.

We are being taught to recognise the siskin,
the dunnock, appreciate the spotted woodpecker
who daily visits our garden birdfeeders, the jays
that swoop our hedges, the fledgling sparrows

chirping in their porch home. We are walking
culm grasslands, treading the spaces between
mature beech, ancient oak and striding conifer.
The camera is my notebook, the notebook

is your camera, the pages are illustrated,
the prose becoming poetic. Tormentil is our
common companion, framing the way for
heather, rushes, gorse and golden saxifrage.

Two collared doves watched us move in,
two collared doves drink, eat and rest
by our kitchen window. We are the visitors,
they are the generations-established residents.

There is a crescent moon in the skies
over the forest tonight. It is waking the foxes,
the red deer, the badgers; it is stirring the owls.
Ruby Country is silent in pregnant light.

We will grow here, in nature and of nature.
We are the words and the eyes.
We are the keepers.
We cannot end this story.

Fallen: to the forest

Hesitant through the pine
trees this morning labouring
slower than canine
cursing the cropped
nature of this wood
weft leeched
into us slyly
stayed by their roots
their ancient verticals.
Every second it takes
to cut, to kill them
is personal.
Our like-loved sap
rises
anticipating later's
inevitable bereavement
a loss too queer
to find adequate counsel.
Slow-shuttered
we keep them
inner-eyed
as imprints
to peel away
like dusty slides
once enjoyed
on Sunday afternoons.

My Moon in Cancer

A mist hangs over the forest today
hiding the already hidden, deadening
sound and spreading rumours of Autumn
to the full-leaf trees, still deep-rooted in Summer.

Our light tracks which crackled through
the broadleaf, hushed through the pine,
are cleansed by unseen water droplets,
floating clouds in gullies and hollows.

It is a day for the trees to stand alone,
for the mosses and grasses to be refreshed,
the wildlife to wander at will without
being startled by invasive intruders.

There is change in the air, anticipation.
The Beech is ready to announce this season's
colours, the Dogwood too. Bog Asphodel
strips its yellow blooms, Campion its pink.

You brought your Cusp of Energy, vibrant,
to meld my Moon in Cancer. Tonight, with
newly-opened eyes, we'll watch this
September moon glow for foragers and hunters.

In our Northern skies Gemini will shine.
Looking South, Orion will tell us
that Autumn is near. Seasons are changing.
Standing here, we know some things never will.

The word in the wood

If I uncurl my dumb ears
and place my face
where it will catch
the first light
breath from Dartmoor
fingering its way over
the down and up
along the track

If I hush the loudness
of the paddock's warming soil
of my crackling bark
and joints
taught with wet March
and ready for more

If I am morning-careful
with green tones,
the cumbersome translations
of xylem
and phloem
an osmosis of man
and plant

I will hear the word,
the delicate word
that one wild
word come
in the wood
as

bud.

Home

Under camera-stars and gossip-trees,
enclosed in the known and love of things,
I can rest informed and protected.

The fussy bee with its golden knees
leaves the Malus to shuffle on my hand
showing me where the buds are appearing.
The emerald dragon hovers iridescent,
happy that the clay pool has refilled.
The pearl-bordered fritillary moved here
for the scabious and loosestrife by the forest
now her old home is empty warehousing.

Away from home private wealth is harboring art.
Away from home a government is denying literature.
Away from home a soldier walks towards us
through a field of dead or dying flowers,
half-buries his rifle, barrel open to the sky,
circles it with red poppies in bare earth
before continuing his search for the perfect rose.

Firs

The firs are bleeding
white sap, wounds in the forest
with sounds of gun shot

Roadford Lake, before we moved

Its bud had been late,
trapped by the slap
of March and wounded.
It had found a catch
of warmth beyond,
the wood's harness,
an irreverence in the
starched congregation
of pines, purse-lipped,
tutting.

Clad in a scab
of last year's cones,
the bough had borrowed
one spit of sun and
like an impatient child
had allowed itself
a liberty of laughter;
exhibiting its earliest
burlesque
as an unembarrassed leaf:
a promise.
It was the first
in the wood
that we'd noticed.

Listen, you said,
it's speaking.

Communing

This open door leads to Dartmoor,
where the I watch the lichen colonize the earth.
I walk this summered skin in frost,
treading gloved mosaics of bramble grasses
and talk to the Anglo-Saxons through mist.

I scrape my fingers on midwinter air,
peel back the centuries' layers, hold close
the rowan tree that leads me to spring.
The snowed Galloway shows me brown on white,
the Scotch Blackface shows me white on white.

My play is the drama of the High Moor
the scenery is the western flank,
the applause is the Dart's flowing thunder.
Flat on the kistvaen's granite capstone
I whisper to my ancestors. They are content.

There is snow dusting, there is sunlight,
there is peat forming beneath my feet.
The soft rush is telling me to pick my tread,
the ley line guiding me to cob and thatch.
The way is blue, over the gold is Cornwall.

I leave my landscape in the hall,
in the orange light I make a poem.
And with your two thumbs on this page,
your index fingers straddling the cover,
I speak to you. I am speaking to you right now.

That bird we could not see

Did you hear that bird
thrill song in a March
afternoon walk after rain
high to the tor
in the distant blue and gold
over the spruce,
the ones that are
still standing?
Did you hear it soar
fast like it was freed
from its cage
and chasing the wind
coming off the sea at Bude,
trying to beat it
for joy and because it could?
Did you recognise
the song from somewhere
primitive and deep
as if you could reply
and try?

You did.
I know it.
My heart did too.

Fragments of the Mystic Moor

i *Releasing The Legends*

The sound of my shoes on shingle,
like legends' chains to the sea;
and the winds through hands of western gorse
and crows squabbling over the scree.

The silence of hawks in the still air,
my breath forming genie-lamp mist;
my mind chasing free by the menhir,
ancestors reliving their myth.

The circle of stones that surrounds me
impregnates the air with the past;
held then by hands of western gorse
until releasing the legends at last.

ii *Near Wistman's Wood*

Wistman's Wood, imposing and proud,
rises at the young Dart's twisting neck,
a sculptured gothic, deformation of sorts.

Mixed generations of granite clitter
are grey evidence of restlessness,
where buzzards hold glad carnival

above a majestically isolated moorland,
as when the druids, too, sought isolation –
peace in the mystic wilds of Dartmoor.

Moor haiku

Listen to the moor –
giants' beards drip through stunted oak
Wistman's poetry

From the Teign Valley

High above the three-arched Fingle Bridge
unseen zephyrs blow warmth to the tumbling Teign
and run with shadows along Fisherman's Path.
We stride and stroll the inclined woods, leaf soft
and pine silent, before the descent of Piddledown Common.
In our cottage acres, the fruit wine holds the sun,

you are barefoot in the stream that thunders the valley
and I am slumped under the old willow, watching you.
I have learned to love the hawthorn, Sisyphus-leaning
on the high moor, scarred against bracken and fern.
I have learned to love this valley, its reaves and woodland,
and this late sun which is holding the day until we are done.

Opus on Exmoor

She flows over
the brightling stones
in grey and white
dripping wet glissandos
between hedge end and nettle-bed,
little pianissimo susurrations
shushing as she passes.

Next to her,
in chorus, and behind,
we stilt blunt riverside staccatos
in beech husk and brown
mud, bouldered and too loud
plucking treble foot
and forte.

In threes
we lean into the measured
timbre of the Lyn
learning the ease
of these wet grace notes
and the fading opus
of a morning moor's
dissolving
diminuendo.

Dartmoor Song

The cloudburst by ancient Pizwell
had failed to muddy the track enough
to stop our boots and paws progressing
and the wind rustled just long enough
to flutter the lungta-style prayer flags
colouring the trees in the Lower Merripit vale,
communing with the hidden shrines
and ceremonial round houses.

The East Dart continued its story
through Bellever and sprayed the old
clapper bridge, designed for carts,
now beloved by catalogues and cameras.
And here I stand, knee-deep in September,
the sun now high and trees dripping apples.
Here you can swallow me whole
or place me with others frozen in time.

Walk me to the rise of King's Tor
then drop me deep in the Walkham Valley.
Trace me the tracks of the Devonport Leat
to the heart of Foxtor Mires and let the call
of the meadow pipit be my only alarm cry.
Leave me here with the silence that haunts,
the heartbeat that feeds my serenity
and the wind that brushes over these words.

The White

The white word has come
from the wood to the west,
licking the cedars, the pines
with a new glaze,
heavy-topped
like barmaids.

It has whispered from the moor,
dying the culm and tuft,
turning churned clay to silent.
It is hushed, top-clothed
reverently laid
like a Lent Bishop.

It has laughed over school yard,
town and motorway,
determining its own
peculiar rules
until we are undone
like poor poets, waiting patients.

And under the dark
it has stolen, pale thief
to dune and beach,
dipping the toes
of its long, lean letters
into the sea
until even the waves' blue fingers
are stopped.

The white has come
from a frozen mouth
with its words,
its quiet revolutions.
Shhhhhhh! Be careful.
Listen.

Summer Evening, Cam Peak

Time's waistcoat watch has halted here.
Cam Peak, seen from the fox-track meadow
high with birthing grass, rising behind two
sides of the church tower, nature's friar
with bald dome and fringed woods.

Ramblers on the summit stand monolith black,
those approaching appear and disappear,
prairie dogs investigating hinterland.
The querulous and the quidnunc don't climb hills;
behind your back is just the walking breeze
and the running wind.

Now I have joined the peak diaspora
from Cam Long Down, Uley Bury, May Hill
and far Black Mountains, the black tinged
with blue from the shadowing of this evening sun
diffused over tessellated counties.

Below is a blue-tractored farmer in his three-green field,
watching another bale roll to the edge.
There's the sleepy hum of a buzzard-sized plane
a full two clouds away; nature has slipped into
Gloucestershire; summer has settled.

I breathe the combined scents of summer evening,
listen to the music that summer evenings play.
A snail has created mirrors in the nettles, purely
to reflect and dance with the sun, proving again
to those who look, your god is in the detail.

quidnunc – gossip, back-stabber

Dress Greening

I had thought of a dress
ready for spring,
too early yet for blue bells
still hidden in green leaf,
but cloth-dotted with stars
of early celandines and rampant
primrose, yellowing the homespun
taken from my wood-walked floor.

I had thought of undergarments,
white snow's drops
with fine green frills,
aconite-bright filaments
to tease the toucher

And turnings of ivy
winding round my waist
through to the skin, held
together with little zips of catkins;
soft slippers too in moss.

And round the neck
(by way of warning)
will be a running briar, unmanageable
except by one who carefully removes
the thorns, perhaps reveals
the pleasure of a rose.

I had thought of a dress
ready for spring –
a cottoning of words to make it.

Over the Malvern Hills

Three of us on the slopes of Summer Hill,
two people and one dog taking the steep path
on this hot day I borrowed from the summer.

You catch the blue I throw towards you
and hold it above any potential cloud;
nothing can spoil this quintessential day.

We rest on the summit of The Beacon,
Great Malvern spread as a cluster diamond
in the tesserae of farms and meadows.

We switch views from Evesham's Vale
to the mountains and valleys of Wales,
cloaked in fitting silence, pierced by buzzards.

Following the secluded Victorian driveway,
hidden Earnslaw Lake appears obsidian,
refusing to reflect the tall neighbour beeches.

Malvern streets resound to minor interruptions,
the heat rising as a mirage below a bronzed Elgar,
permanently watching over his favoured café.

In the seclusion of our room, we hear the music
serenading those seated around the parks bandstand;
we hear evensong from the adjacent Priory.

We have time-travelled this perfect weekend,
doing whatever was then, what is now,
doing whatever our hearts thought was easy.

Being There

On the morning-moist edge of Chase Woods
fallen conkers are protected in their
green sputnik cases, lying in a firebed
of wounded autumn leaves. Under the rising sun

the trees are black; to each side a painter
has daubed the canopy with diffused orange.
My dog is a steam train running against
a barrage of birdsong. I'm a margin of nostalgia
in some spent photograph.

The sloping rows of blackcurrants drop an arc
to the meadow, the gaps between shining
as warming ice, as dew and light live their
daily awakening. There is a reproduction of shadows
in this molten waving motion of vision.

On this church-chime Sunday, it doesn't
matter if we loved once; it doesn't matter
if we've never met; it doesn't matter if our
paths will never cross again. What matters
is that when I exhale this, you sense the air,

my breath the failing breeze you feel.
When I look to the far spire you too will see
across the fields with me, there on the book
in your hand, on every single wall you own,
in whatever direction you care to look.

It's the only important thing this ennobled moment:
Being there.

Misty Morning, Hildersley Fields

It feels eerie here on this muted chiming Sunday,
with the silvered waving horizon feathering sight.
Two stout trees, formed like weathered Yorkshiremen
stand guard to one edge of the faltering wood,
appearing and vanishing with perfidious profligacy.

The small oak bears the scattered ashes
of once-running dogs, who emerge on days like these,
to play again, enjoy the scents of happy trails
and burst the hearts of those left behind,
the devastated souls of devoted masters.

Corn stubble beckons yellow through the white,
stunted vague Van Gogh with sounds of footsteps.
Here too are the smoky conversations of death-or-glory
soldiers, billeted and waiting for the foreign fields
of 1940, in bucolic beauty prior to battles.

No crosses here, but late wild poppies
bleeding into the soil, watched over by the
land-girl crops of new generation farmers,
watched over by the wood's intricate creatures,
their nacreous eyes holding this Sunday still enough
for the strolling love of one man and his dog.

Dorset Evensong

Up to our ankles in large sand
as the late lap of September
presses people homewards
from West Bay's beach

we can hear the trills
of hidden fossils, flint-sharp
syncopations, secrets burning
wanting to be plucked and rung

we are learning their long patois
tongued-tied with the newness
of days' ancient clicks and clatters
an impatient jangling of eras

as the sun sets

they rattle their song past
our hammers, our useless taps
so belemnites and ammonites
might have their way

we'll stop, we'll wait,
perhaps we'll catch the wisdoms
waiting in this prehistoric
evensong.

On emerging fragrantly from the WC at Lyme Regis

Today I will despise
those still fertile women
with refined rumps
who can squeeze between
sanitary disposal unit
and the razor sharp teeth
of the toilet roll dispenser
applying their compliant
softparts on to the arctic climes
of a stainless steel receptacle
masquerading as a loo seat
whose pert message
to *pee cleanly*
has almost rubbed off
(through improper use)
and, because the hooks
on which to hang shopping,
leads or handbags have disappeared
for safety reasons,
can juggle such things
on their laps, or heads
(depending on agility)
and then actually pluck themselves
from the vacuum, the frost of stuck metal
(fixed and double bolted –
for fear of theft),
in order to encounter
the petulant handwashing system
which soaps, wets and blows
(but not necessarily in that order)
to emerge fragrantly refreshed
and serene
because, sorry, agreed (like the sign),
OUT OF ORDER.

Crackington Haven

The pebbles point fingers to the cliffs
whose contour faces lead to the sea.
Here in Gaia's birthing pools we are lulled
by the song of silver-paper water,
a solo for many voices, patterned by tree-light,
scented by the green promise of East Wood.

We walk with shadows of Clare, Frost and Marlowe,
see through their eyes the cushioning moss trail
crushed to jeweled droplets by our thirsty boots
until we emerge blinking into new light,
surfacing with the wild goats whose trackways
lead uninitiated to the fierce fall of Cambeak.

We respect the treachery of wind-edged boulders
until the welcome harmony of sea and sand,
where the white breakers are cleaning the canvas
of footprints and paws, smoothing anew
for tomorrow's paddlers and painters who are
waiting in anticipation and holiday sandals.

On things we cannot know
Gentle Jane

After another wet day
we take to the beach
for a late trickle of s u n

Down the slate track
from our borrowed home,
past the gypsy caravan,   beyond.

He's cracking slate,   s k i m   m ing
between ball-bouncing
for a dog that's loved twice.

His patience peels us both,
making hard layers
become known, soft,   opened.

He smiles,   above me,
talking of the dozen swans
he's seen again   and heard.

They are singing of things
we cannot know he says.
Perhaps   in the shift   we can.

Padstow Spring

Thank you John Worden for letting us use your bench.
It's hot, John, and we've walked miles on the sand.
It says on your plaque you were a Padstow Caroller:
this morning I thank you for the Irish busker,
who doesn't know me from Adam, but is choosing to sing
Dylan's 'Girl From The North Country' as if a request.

We'll just sit here for a while. We're breathing
the sea and watching the seagulls squabbling
on the deck of Grumpy B, the mast of Flying Sue
and around the hull of Annie Callie. Cormorants
are finding that far too busy for this idle day.
I have my lady's head on my shoulder, my collie

damp and sandy, lying at our feet. We've sat on the rocks,
written the cards in a cove we found, beat the incoming tide.
Now we're in the postcard John, thanks to your bench.
I just have to bottle this feeling, seal in this longing,
to pour over us when others choose to sit here
on our timeless shadows, two people and a sleeping dog.

Hawkers Cove

near winter

Last night's tide
has left soft sand
enough for us both
to sink into.

I walk behind
taking your steps
one at a time
striding long-legged
more than is easy
leaving no trace
fitting your places
completely
invisible other than you
as if I had not walked
and was not
not even beached
only one shadow
in a long winter sun.

I am made wraith
here as you breathe
eagerly inhaled
unseen consummately,
utterly unborn

watching whilst being
swallowed.

Early year view

Here in my slow
cup of rock
I will trade spray
with rain, fret
with fog, the black spew
of mussel beards
sooting my seat.
Shells grow quietly
as love given later.
When I watch you
I am finding days
I have yet to spend
and burying them inner;
mollusc-like.
I want to double knot
this view, this secrecy
around your year's waist,
remind you
under cloud,
within everything like us,
the best is waiting.

It's as you left it, John

It's as you left it John.
The green Olympia typewriter
next to the brown telephone
on the four-drawer bureau desk.
I fingered the round pad keys,
formed the words *Senex* and *Trebetherick*
It's now in Wadebridge John,
where you once observed from its station
that the sea scented the Camel Valley.

We came to see you John,
took the cliff path from Polzeath,
walking above the Vinnick Rocks and round
to Daymer Bay, which, suited and white-fedora'd,
was your own pre-stroke stroll.
The sand was indeed golden and vast houses
told of the nearness of Rock and its money.
We found a circular path around Brea Hill
and crossed a stream. We were there, John.

St Enedoc, oasis of the fairway,
silent except for gulls, and reverential.
Your scrolled gravestone, just the name,
with no 'Sir' inscribed, no fitting verse.
Dawn entered the church, I sat above
your grave, recited the off-by-heart
Myfanwy in my head, though struggled
through the more obscure *Myfanwy at Oxford.*

We left you by the shells and bladderwrack.

Mr Cox's Monterey Pines

That man who once painted
the second coming with
clear renaissance skies
across the chapels or salons
of the godly and rich,

I wonder if he
would have captured
with his fine brush
and sharpened eye,

given the pure
golds and ochres
from Lascaux,
the swirls, the butter-coloured
stratas and impromptu lilacs
made by Pliny or Vermeer,

I wonder if even he
would have fashioned
with centuries of clever hands
and perfect tints
what even your camera
will not trade:

the glory of the time
and turn of this used sun
dropping on the rocks
with eight rooks crossing
the frilled Camel
over a bar and beach,
safe to the tops of
Mr Cox's Monterey Pines.

Seven rocks

The seven rocks in my pocket
have stopped being heavy.
They are a cairn
away from this beach
I once loved
more than my mother;
that pressed salt and sea
into the sole of a child,
bottom up
until it could breath
like a fish
away from its shoal.

They will mark
the height of the cliff,
the wet of a loaded wave,
the colour of a father
as he swims all day
waiting for a four-year girl
and her sister to learn
how to join him.

They will be the rough
lump in the throat
on a last day swallow,
the Chapel Porth hill,
the chest's poor hollow,
the mine in the cliff
leading the car down
to a three-week borrow.

I will roll their killas,
their schist,
the mantle of their bold
bones until sparks fly
or runes can be cast
fired with land slip
and whetstone filing
my rivers down
to the sea's lip.

Balmaidened,
their flint will be offspring
to my mother's rock:
scars and sweetmeats,
to my four years,
up to my all-decades waiting:
these seven rocks,
these true rocks,
these mind-in-my hand
that made me
scroll and covenant
rocks brought from the beach
at Porthtowan.

'Killas' is a Cornish mining term for metamorphic rock.

Lerryn Creek

We listen to the midsummer quiet,
no lap, no rustle, no talk, no breeze –
just us two perched on granite boulders,
away from the bank, as the tidal creek slowly fills.

This silent green-black water is inching over mud
creating circular ripples, like invisible rain
falling on this hottest of June days,
buried life responding to its liquid dressing.

A circular shape of glass-light,
streaked with dark from Ethy Woods,
drifts across the surface, bank to bank,
glinting the sky back to its source.

The summer sound of an indistinct bird
meets two people mapping out words
in their heads, a dog nosily treading
over gradually darkening gravel.

The stepping stones are covered now,
so we cross over by the old bridge,
stand to take a last look at the watercolour
we've left, now kayaked and reflective.

The world has left us for a while, all we need
is here. In this remote place between Cornwall's
high hedges, we become new shadows
in the silent serenity of Lerryn Creek.

Sitting at Lerryn Creek

Like a slow summer thought
she seeps, a shy offspring
leaking a flat path
up the creek to-ing
her way from Fowey.

The trickle ribbon
scalpels the silt.
There will be time
to stay with it today.

If I stand on rock
and cup my ear
I can hear answers
for you in the drift
rising like bubbles;
words from the mud.

I have pulled weed
from the rough banks
until a tree-line lies
straight. We'll wait
for a fro-ing to purge.

I'll ask you to lean
on this tide
as your days come,
to wait, to watch
for a river,
the one that has yet to run.

Trebah Remembered

"To Remember Me Just Look Around" ~ Eira Hibbert, 1917-2009

Not spare or mean
this May garden
pressing its green limbs
down to the sea,

lavish like a birthday
guest with parcels
of bark, of fern,
of flower and bud,

tipsy with maple
wine beech and lipstick
pinked rhododendrons
loudly gunnera,

toasting Alice and Eira
with Tepa, Hiba, Acer, Palm,
whose soaked roots
rose-daughtered, nurtured

to this most beautiful wound
in Helford's granite,
weeping only waterfall
and walks, not war now,

for those who wander
down the recollected paths
of Trebah.

That day in the promise of my youth

That day in the promise of my youth
I heard *And Death Shall have No Dominion*
My first witness of such trailing words
Beautiful
I sought out the name
Child eyes opened by the conjuror of this verse
My age just a fragile ten, my stature holistic
Soaring by peers
Rising with the stirring in my unhewn mind

The flow that was the sound of Dylan Thomas
Covered my boundaries now smudged into poems
Striving hard and falling through beauty
Sensual
And full of music
Carrying young nostalgia and reminiscence
Poetry's majesty chiselling in my heart
Never to waiver
Inspiring
This power that captures my daydreams and guides my sight

My soul had been made aware of the unknown
And the tower of sounds that could roll from the tongue
My new birth from the visionary
Beautiful
Passion and sorrow
Guiding my future through *The Colour of Saying*
My pen and latterly keyboard lilting inadequate
Satiating pure thought
Exploring
The strident colours of my mind's own land.

On finding a piece of blood red gabbro

Did you draw those quick skies
of wax crayon blue
broken only by a circle
sun, a face with rays
at 3, and 6, at 9 and 12

Did you draw only straight trees
in symmetry and balanced
leaves in sequence set
in the pointy, alternated bed
of five-stalked grass

Did you ruler the sand flat
when giving every page
its yellow-only beach
and sea with waves,
each neat in formation lines of w

Or could your brilliant eyes
ink curves even then,
swirl clouds of cumulus and cirrus
and trees irregular and angled
with complications then of twig, of bark

And did your sand, my loved foot-fellow,
have large names even then
like gneiss and schist,
of tremolite and serpentine?
And in the picture filled with weeks
did you always find

on drawing days
a piece of blood red gabbro.

The End of Summer

The End of Summer is seated in the subtle lounge
of Mole's Cottage in the Manor courtyard.
Mole is vividly painted, hung with wind-chimes,
which play melody to Vettriano's Singing Butler.

It is resting awhile on the blind seals at Gweek,
freeing the bones of the elderly adventurers,
drying the sand of the younger moat-builders
casting long shadows in minds and hearts.

The End of Summer is wandering by the slipway,
passing the leisure boats and sky-bright sails,
lighting the wooded slopes of Frenchman's Creek,
the mud and creeping saltwater of Helford Passage.

It is saying goodbye to ancient Lowland Point,
having a last hurrah with Coverack's child-leaping harbour,
waiting to close the cash-cottage doors and tuck
the village into a winter-long blanket of emptiness.

The End of Summer is winding Rosenithon lanes
to the sea, where hidden Godrevy Cove lures the season
to crash on the water-buried Manacle Rocks,
paving the way for Autumn's safe arrival.

It is joining us in the sea, wrapping bladderwrack
around paddling ankles, creating juvenile waves
and songs to orchestrate the memory of days,
the stirring of nights, the end of the summer.

Burn

Bright brands today
gamboge and cadmium
blazing over the Roseland
in celandine
and daffodil drift.

We have hurt eyes.

Fire beacons of gorse
singe the tops
shouting bud love
into the air's lust,
dropping clothes
of dandelion, cowslip,
coy primrose.

We burn without sun.

Led down the path
to undercover Towan
mother-die lies
quiet, in wait,
keeping its curled
many-headed infants
close and clever
yellow unspent.

We wait for time:
its astonishing salve.

I was there

Towans Beach

Yes, I was there
and the sea was that blue and
the sky sly-creeping in
cold over from France
to the day-warm sand.

Yes, I did hear
the villain-voice of the tide
as it crept up to Place's
dunes where you, unhidden
were child, shadow-bowling.

Yes, I did feel the wet
peppering of the sand-dog
over-legged and yapping
at pebbles, tree, weed,
imaginary beach-sprites, loved.

And yes it was me looking,
cutting the troubles,
the glum stutterings of others,
with a shutter's click
simply for me, as a marker.

Timing

Not when the cars come past
at speed on Sunday mornings
followed by three brainless motorcycle
riders bent on out-pillocking
each other past our trees.
Not when George is drilling
into metal parts of another
damned shed
ensuring the titanium
is secure from possible nuclear attack,
or Paul trying to bomb his way
into his own lounge SAS-style
with trumpet accompaniment.
Not when John is cutting bricks
to lay his path in another direction
or Ringo singing like a Valkyrie
with metal-roofed drums.
Not when the trees fall,
the lightning strikes or the
thunder bellows its bass
through the stumps funnels.
Not even when the mower starts,
the hoover bites, the septic tank tilts
or the pans fall like boulders
out of Booby-trap Cupboard.

But when the wind has stopped,
the electricity ceased
and the jobs declared complete;
when the eyelids, heavy
rest like a heart on slow and
one leaf laden lets
its little self   fall,

                 that's when the bugger decides to bark.

Whilst Bathing Virginia Woolf's Back

Her back is arched for me to soap.
'I bathe with my eyes closed' she says.
'But I can't see your eyes that way.' I complain.
'The eyes of others are our prisons.' she replied.
Fair enough, I thought.

'I'm writing a poem in the soap bubbles' I advise,
tell her the water's turning the 'O's to 'Q's,
words changing, but the essence still there.
'The poet gives us the essence, prose takes the mold
of the body and mind.' Fair enough, I thought.

With the random words leaking, I sign 'Anon'
and prod a full stop. She asks me to stop prodding her.
'You have signed it Anon I feel, so you must be a woman.'
She thought I was a woman– and she's naked.
'What is your name?' 'Daisy Carruthers' I offer.

I leave before she glimpses this bearded imposter.
Virginia gropes for a towel, I dash to tell Dawn.
'You'll never guess who I've written soap poetry with…'
but I couldn't get her attention. She was preoccupied:
euphorically painting in the Michael Bublé life class.

Man waiting
at The Hurst

There's an old man listening
as I balance the shy white
cloud of my room,
holding on to the sides
before it tips over.

It is too heavy tonight.
There is a pile of cry
dancing under my skin and
my words are bulging barrels
with a nine month ache.

I'm looking to smell a sound
but my head is full of bees.
I wait for today's wine bonnet
to warm me, let it slip me,
fall, bounce me to a dream
belonging to someone else.

– Boys in grey wool shirts,
pink knees matching the apples of their cheeks.
They are muddied, jumping up at mirrors,
struggling with caps.
I have their mud between my feet.

– Big-tongued gypsy women
in red and orange skirts,
whose lips can open oysters
and sing beautiful cacophonies.
They give me pearls to hold in my teeth.

– A girl with torn hair and rattled eyes
screaming at me through the haar.
We hold and bang the walls
together, like square balls
rubbering the sterile cleanness.
She's looking for the face I think I have lost.

There's an old man waiting
when I wake wet-faced, running
in my bed past morning.
He's willow backed
between the trees, holding
a canvas sack of silver squirrels'
caps, shells and tears.
He smiles. He disappears.

Maybe I know him.
Maybe he's been here before.
Maybe, one day, I'll need him again.

Transcendental

A mind is like a parachute. It doesn't work until it's open ~ Frank Zappa

I was trying to put a song in another's mouth.
My skin was white, one layer down it was black.
My skin was all shades of brown. It was beautiful
and irrelevant. I became universal for a few months
less than a year and was collecting the words I'd dropped.

I worked gently, careful not to bruise or distort.
If I held too tightly, people would argue in a country
I'd never heard of. If I squeezed fists over them
war would be declared in a country I'd never heard of.
I rubbed as many as I could onto parchment,

let my blood flow through my isolated mind
where it pulsed freely over future memories.
I held it to the sun and slowly tore, its shine flooding
the peeled 'V' and my words rose like summer.
Many years later I reattached the parchment

and heard the whispers soar through centuries.
I used to just know, but now I believed –
the collected words had given their colours
to others or fallen to oceans where, when you listen,
they emerge as a song I put in a whale's mouth.

The Light Fandango

Thin life-scratches hiss from a Dansette
and we rise in tipsy awkwardness
with that dance of colour and fire,
that dance of smoke and ice.

We peel our skin and leave
on the back of the door
for others to admire,
while we rub bones
and you choose to float through me.
I freeze erect at how
that passion could have been.

I asked you how it felt
to be one of the beautiful people?
"I'm happy to be that way" you reply,
smiling at the distance of another song.

"It feels like fire and ice,
like all colours rising."
We leave the cartwheels for others
while we watch the room spin with people
who are wearing our skin
and look exactly like us.

In India

i. Calangute

In India, I listened.
He was yellow and gold
and pilgrims sat cross-legged
to absorb each word
that spiralled in light.

He drew a map of my life
so clearly in the sand.
I understood the goals,
the man that lay within,
my single sense of purpose.
I understood each direction,
the eventual result,
the road not taken.
It was so pure, so clear.

I scooped the map
into my back-pack
and carried it throughout
my sandalwooded journey,
physical and spiritual,
until I felt lost, alone.

I tipped out the map
onto sacred marble,
then searched the sand
for the sign that read
'You Are Here'

ii. Anjuna

Toes picked through sand and sought shade,
inner peace was a constant, teachings
were temple and mountain, the light
glowing in my head revealed secret blemishes.

Carrying the mystic where we could,
freed from responsibility in this youthful time,
I'd been told I would make it, absorb naturally,
unravel the pure mystery and achieve enlightenment.

The beach held between sandal and foot,
I was Kaftan and Kameez, linen, cotton.
I was cheesecloth-white, no clothes,
no expectation or boundaries or harm.

It couldn't last, it wouldn't last, but walking
through bamboo, led by kite and kestrel,
it didn't matter. The counter-culture
was someone else's word, another's song.

For now, young and sun-held, I was
inspired just by existing among the joss,
the cardamom and cinnamon, the music
and people, the scents and sense of my life.

I still see the waters, smell forest, feel my sweat.
I still hear an acoustic guitar bounce from stars
where we shared strange smoke, shared like-minds.
We held the day, each other, nothing more.

The remains of someone else's fire

The remains of someone else's fire
look lost and spurned,
the damp within the wood
having won and lost
its ardour to coax
a flame, ignite
a late-night purpose.

The remains of someone else's fire
grate-waits, defeated
cold-cast until a hand,
more careful with craft
and heart, will brush
the burn to tease a spark,
enable that once charred
bough to flame again,
perhaps to glow,
perhaps, if fanned,
to roar.

In my skull's cave

She holds my hand while sleeping,
as I lie beneath my mask of cold air,
contact safety in wherever she's dreaming.
She rests in my skull's cave until morning
where she'll wake behind my eyes.

She wears red socks inside walking boots
as she sits content on her granite boulder
and with the movement of her green pen,
catches the wild in her bible notebook
until freeing it onto the page as a poem.

We walk a perfect day with Polperro painters
along stone-white cobbles and canvas,
this trinity of two legs, two legs, four legs.
weaving alleyways to the harlequined harbour.
Tonight she will hold my hand while sleeping
and in the morning she'll wake behind my eyes.

This is true

This is true:
just as my small finger
seeks the curl of yours
in the cold night
to find the beat, beat, beat
of you living,
I know it is
the drum
that rhythms me daily,
and as I sleep, sleep, sleep
can finally sleep,
I am dancing to it.

She is made

She is made of stone,
pocket-gathered from Chynhall's Point
and trodden by her summer shoes
in the shadow of selected Cornwall.

She is made of bone,
harvested from the sea at Coverack
and hand-picked from wet baskets
in the sparkle of sky-blue boats.

She is made of skin,
love-bound from the earth's mantle
and browned by breezes
in the towering whisper of her sun.

She is made of water,
lapped from the Lizard reed beds
and poured high to the jagged coast
in the pain of space between the sea.

She is made of bell-heather,
spore-borne from Dartmoor's winds
and trodden by her thirsty boots
in the awe of Cox Tor's circle.

She is made of wood,
earth-given from Neolithic farmers
and garnished by green filigree
in the druid majesty of Wistman's Wood.

She is made of air,
ingested from familiar skies
and colourful as Dublin doors
in the poetry of her waking mind.

Trauma
9th February 2020

This was the morning I woke
entombed in ice and saw
through the stifled window
that flowers were lowering their heads
and the forest blew hollow.

This was the morning she rose
her mind probing night's dark work,
summoning those who would turn
my prison to mist above new light
allowing me to meet the morning.

Weeks later I was warm again,
released to walk the early forest.
She made this happen because
she reflected our future in her eyes
and carried summer in her cupped hands.

Two capital letters

Before we were such upright I's
all flat-top, straight and big-footed
readysteady, to go places.
We leaned, were props or propped
occasionally slipping,
knocked flat or
bedded.

Now we are bent S's
curlshouldered, rumped
or tummied in that round ample
way that life-times give.
We hook, catching each other,
tangled hangers, joined
weight bearing.

And blue ...
A poem for her birthday

And blue was

The six-year-old's favourite dress,
with white scalloped collar,
flaring enough when she spun
and worn on high days and holidays.

The lollipops that stained her tongue
on sunny days; the gingham ribbon,
tight on disobedient hair; the bruise
that faded with her mind's rising.

Morning-escape Chynhalls Point ocean;
her own child's fingers, cold in the ripples
of the wave lace that bound them;
the ink of her poem, helping her breathe;

And blue is

The flash of jays' feathers across
her forest garden; the flower of the green
alkanet that borders the wood; the River
Dart's reflective mirror at Bellever.

The Camel Estuary, whose siren was heard
by her children, their spouses, to travel
the miles to join us, be close to her skin
and plot the Padstow-Rock birthday surprises.

Her song by Joni Mitchell
with a shell that holds a sigh;
      my song by Bob Dylan
      that she's so happily tangled up in.

Blue Drift

Quarried like granite
dug out diamond
or unlucky opal,
you have exposed
a vein in me
that is brighter,
more luminous
than any prospector told.

The stone freed,
has been knocked,
chipped, ground
between boulders
to its mica.
That which seemed
sea glass or feldspar
has become a surprised sapphire

gathered in the hand
of a man
walking at tide-time
in flotsam.

And leaning

Some days, when the sun drops
and I am looking for blood
to unstiffen me,
journey me onwards;

when the thin soul
is struggling over banks and ditches,
nettles tickling its throat to tears,
and cries, buried in sets, in dens;

I will lean against you,
your hands holding, warming
my heart's weight,
thawing my hurt with braced wrists.

Even at night, when the cold creeps,
only a palm pressed against
your chest's rise and firm deep
is enough to heat me, perhaps find relief.

It is a curious stitching,
this mixture of love and leaning.

It is right

It is right that the last light
should catch your face
on this winter's day
as you rest late in the fire
of an evening

Because you have freed
the lost bees struggling
in a string of sheds,
the moth pleated into the folds
of a sudden morning

Because you have rescued
the worm from dug clay,
unstruck the ruffled chaffinch,
harboured donkey, goat and pig,
rescued innumerable chickens,
and me

But mostly because lately
you have scooped our baggy-limbed dog
into places he could not otherwise be,
tenderly, definitely, collie-hearted
keeping your pack close

and I have seen it.

It is right that the last light
should catch your face
on this late winter's day
as you rest late by the fire,
loved in an evening.

Making incense

The tabernacle will call again:
rock laid upon rock,
wood upon wood
in this birded communion.

Your particular incense:
three white hairs from a coat,
calvados, hemp and rose pot-pourri,
corn heads and vanilla, I rise up

My unusual offering
to the kind goddess who once
painted my cold body blue
and called you, bent you

To me, my saving.

No mad wode now
just a leaf cure and fine
smoke, ambered joss burning
from a hearth healed
letting us make
incense.

Senryu at Leicester Square

Christmas gift for him
Chinatown spice and sweet hoard
cake-crumbs in her bra

Kitchen Manoeuvres

She is making lemon curd.
I watch her busying her lemons,
arranging the expectant jars.
Eggs, butter, caster sugar,
zest and juice, whisks, blender,
heavy pan will all be put to use.

All stand to attention under her fingers,
aromas of the act she's controlling
fill the room with anticipation.
"I've just heard one pop" she grins,
holding her gingham-topped creation
and oh, that feeling......that feeling.

Free medlars

I tell you to wait
for the medlars
a little longer
than usual this year.
I want them
to be pitted
as well as sugar brown
and bletted ready
to fall just
as the wasps come.

The old fat ones
will make the sweetest jelly.

Pan brewed
and witch strained
the blooded liquor
will stick you to it
in amber
your beard preserved
with rouge juice
as tough to remove
as history.

In the lane

There wasn't time
to make a child. Late
we'd come to it
and void-wombed.
We'd already loved four.

Instead we formed
bodies in willow,
rowan-armed, beech-legged,
fern-swaddled

silver poplar
through their early hair;
soft-clothed
in spindrift like gypsies.

They ran like leats,
endless and undying,
singing like finches
in a home hedge.

This was our other seed,
our other sap and planting.
Our best, our very best of us,
their unheard whistle, our strong song.

I wait for them
in the sometimes lane –
you in front, me behind –
echoed tread and missing:

the four we loved,
the four we didn't have.

Poem about a scarf

I wanted to ask you for a scarf,
stitched and twisted together to form
an easy circle that would not slip.

I wanted it to be crimson red, crumpled
where it had once been pinchpenny and tight,
where it now laughed loudly in the breeze.

I wanted it to have thread holes
where it had been scuffled on for picnics;
a coverlet when the travelling was cold,

with beaded tassels and hippy
sounds, like little metal leafs or fish
whispering, mouthing as we walked and danced.

I wanted it to have been worn once
by a gypsy, a mother, a child,
and to leak rose joss all through the windings.

I wanted someone to have chosen it
in my favourite colour, someone who knew me,
full of sea and soft with knits & purls.

And I want to ask for it now, as I step
into this year with you, no longer looking
sideways or backward in our forest,

just asking you to pass me a scarf.

Winter Day, Forest Houses

Today my door is a field gate to the paddock,
the carpet is patchy green hit over with mud
trodden by the busy boots of my lady
journeying from the dug earth to the polytunnel.

Her straight lines of obedient onions and shallots
mingle with my unruly crowd of peppers,
still fruiting despite late summer's greenfly army
draining life-juice from the leaves and stems.

'We've more chilli peppers than the Taj.'
I'm told, more forethought required next year.
Linking arms we wellie-walk back to the house,
the chasing collie black, white and newly clay.

We planted a dozen or so trees this year –
right beside the forest. We've interspersed
the hardy with the risky, my drooping willow
enticed by her blousily beautiful Tai Haku cherry.

I go back later to clear up the day and send errant
secateurs back to their hook, turn the wheelbarrow
so any Devon rain will run off. All is secure,
most is still, just the wood settling as light fades.

A muzzle-nuzzle on my hand tells me
someone has snuck out the gate to fetch me.
We thlop through the mud, crunch gravel together.
Boots off in the hall, dog-towel on paws, home.

Preserving
To Chrissy Rogers

Chrissy from over the road
and me on step-stools
skinning onions with butter knives,
crusts in our mouths and tears:
slaves for threepence
and sneering at people
who used spoons instead
(which would never work).

We are Angel Clare and Tess touching
fingers in water bowls
with roots and peeled skins
shrivelling until
all warmth had gone
and feeling; knees
numbed from leaning.

My mother told us
pickles would keep us sharp
(and quiet), weaning me
on their sour malt
until her sweetness left
and I forgot.

Me now with my year's
pink shallots, plump
like gobstoppers
in two glass jars,
the air sharp with acid brown;
their alchemy found,
still preserved.

Walking Through My Family

Solitude here in the winter forest: a single crow
making bare branches aware of my presence,
collie gliding over emerald moss, silent pads,
the hollow where we've stopped free from sounds.

I love it here; it's where many daily walks end,
absorbing the spirit and inhaling the essence,
before returning on a different track; home
of magpies and jays, cackling life we know well.

This is a place to walk through my family.
They appear inside my head and travel a while:
my father with his son, watching our football team,
burning gravy from meat pies staining our hands;

my mother making car parts with fingers made for knitting,
finding late happiness alone in her south-west home;
my sister cycling to a friend on her Pink Witch bike
ready for her first dance, glad her brother has grown;

I watch my daughter walking from nervous first school
to novice mother: twice experienced and still growing;
I walk past a chair that prematurely emptied a few
January's ago: a son who let go of my hand too soon.

The pale sun is burning fire along the bracken path.
I walk through this fire and listen to my boots crackle
the way home. I've had good company, alone, today.
I'll wait for my lady to return, tell her what she's missed.

And Soon, The Rainbow

For my sister Gloria

Some days I'm reminded of you
by the prisms that cover me.
I can call you via the crystals
that define your days, your confidence
through topaz, your truth through verdite;
obsidian countering any negativity.

Your life is curled around you now,
like the ivy around the lightning tree
at the top of our childhood drive
as we waited to see which parent
would be the first to arrive home:
one meaning the night may be turmoil,
the other meaning it may be easy and slow;
nights when one small hand held another.

In your Cornwall you look to the river
but breathe the sea, harness the power
when you watch the moon.
Your dreams are so near.
They are visible, now mists have lifted.
In your hand you hold the colours,
and soon, the rainbow.

Late evening, Veryan

We steal the last squeeze of evening
sun, *the sweetest time*, he'd said
inspecting the extra that was
given and the treat of
ease in the late days
left.

My father garnered these minutes
like wheat ears, rubbing them
until the dusk fell;
like coins, enjoying the gathering,
the shaky-handed jangling
of them in his pockets
later.

His face turned sunward,
he was ruddy,
the colour of apples and sky
as the autumn sun falls –
his sweetest time
I find
now
mine.

Sunday haiku

Him and her on Sunday –
Acker Bilk and Youth Dew
my lost whippoorwills

Painting straight lines

When she was seventeen
my mother learned
how to lean back
and paint a line
down the full length of her
tea-stained leg
with spit and boot black
tattooing a stocking
well enough to persuade
each visiting airman
to give away a portion
of themselves,
snagging herself a catch.

She turned her back
into an impossible arc
open-legged open,
saying her trade any way
was straight
as a line,
not made on flesh
but bread, sugar, silk, wine
enough to allow her
world to unbend,
until she could stand
high-heeled ready
and upright –
her particular victory.

The Grange
for Rita Steward

The corridors smell faintly of impending dinner,
always the same smell, always a different menu.
She sits with others against the wall, her third location,
now further into the room and still not settled.

The diminutive, delightful Filipina arrives.
'Hello, do you want Pasty or Mit Loff?'
'Pasty or what?' 'It's meat loaf' I offer.
'It's not. She said *mit loff*. I'll have that please.'

The tri-lingual Filipina smiles at me and moves on.
On the large-screen TV suspended on the wall
Jeremy Kyle is thankfully inaudible, his silent
gestures ridiculous, but still he attracts vacant stares.

The gentleman opposite sips watered whisky
tells me he was a pilot during the war.
He pauses to hurl unnecessary abuse
at someone who doesn't know she's moaning.

Next to him a lady relives loop memories
with no-one. 'John always came Mondays,
sometimes I'd cook for him, mmmm....'
I wonder if John comes now, Mondays or ever.

I leave, you stay with her for another half-hour.
'You smell lovely' I'm told when kissing goodbye.
'I see with my nose now and you smell lovely.'
I walk the dog over water meadows. The sun is warm...

We carry our sons

We carry our sons
on our shoulders
balancing their weight
until we are bone-grooved
permanent rails in granite.

We carry them
against our spines, splinted,
forcing them to stand,
to walk, fall only lightly,
to peep, tip headlong into love.

We carry them in our blood,
filling our weakling hearts
with their beat, or half-beat
or missing beat, arrhythmic
to our essential syncopation.

We carry them bellied,
both mothered and fathered
by their kicks and turns,
birthing their pain
in entwined family cauls.

The boys we are given
live in our legs, as men in our fists;
their shouts filling our mouths,
their loud, brave song
still as clear as a muezzin.

We have sent our sons,
our beautiful sons,
over tors, too far now
to recognise their scent.
Empty-handed we are still
left wearing the mark
their shape, their weight
easy like a dazzling scar.

Make this poem whole again
for Darren who let go of my hand too soon

Make this poem whole again.
It has become ragged with feeling
and my eyes have diluted the words.
It used to be black and white,

wrought through thirty-two years,
riven with a trembling strength.
It needs a seamstress to hold
it's distant edges together

with invisible thread found
in the Dartmoor leats,
on the Lizard's serpentine back
and deep inside me.

Search for Indigo way down
where myth and mystic meet
in the thin veils of Wistman's
Wood and the Crazywell Pool.

Meld memory and hope
down on Daymer Bay,
bind it with marram,
protect it with gorse.

Please, make this poem whole again,
so I feel warm when it walks with me
draws happy sadness when I read
and always holds this sweetest pain…

Winter breviary

Because I once read
that if a name was said
over again, and over –
through the night and meant –
that person would return,

I have spent the dark
speaking those lost things
with all my heart,
placing them on a spiked tree
as warm bright lights

to surprise you.
No winter in thinking
of living fur, and soft talc
with hairspray, cider,
Christmas dates and whisky-breath.

Me and my quiet choir
shall sing their names
as an antiphon to rouse them,
to bring them back
in a winter breviary.

Do you see? Do you hear?
I have raised them yet.

Walking in the Forest Picture

At this hour of the evening forest
we walk in the sunlight between trees,
notice that shadows are no longer cold
and spring is now leaning towards summer.

In the stillness of the land-locked hill,
we see the field cottages below,
waiting to sleep off another day
and welcome back with orange neon.

We run down the hillside like children,
pretending we're both out of control
until stopping at the stile for breath.
Back up the hill the forest is vague,

no sound now of our crackling footsteps,
no voices where we studied moss-bark,
nothing to say we passed through like spring,
at this hour of the evening forest.

Serendipity is planning my future

The air was shouting storms to the pavement
and the pavement bounced the rain in reply;
the sea was forming waves on this darkest of days
and there was evil brewing under the sky.
The day was made of barbed wire fences
and the grey was scowling over the smiles;
I was caught between me and who I could be
and my journey here was seeming futile.

The night can call the dead from their sleeping,
to walk between the spaces in time;
shadows play host to your mind and a ghost
dressed in white and perfecting the mime.
But here comes the sun in the morning
bearing hope in a heavy disguise;
Serendipity is planning my future
and tomorrow is a perfect surprise.

Acknowledgements

Both authors wish to thank the editors of the magazines in which some of these poems have featured previously, in a number of forms. In a world that needs poetry more than ever, we appreciate all of you and the boost your magazines and on-line forums provide to the creative community.

'The Light Fandango' won first prize in the Poetry Kit Spring Poetry Competition 2019.

'We carry our sons' was first published in *These Are The Hands*, NHS anthology 2020, Fair Acre Press, raising money for NHS Charities Together Covid-19 Emergency Fund.

To the many members of our poetry family who have cajoled, nagged and otherwise hinted for many years that we should combine our voices in a collection – thank you. It worked. Shush now!

With grateful thanks to Louisa Thomsen Brits for giving us permission to use a line from her beautiful collection, *Path* and to Linus for the gift of it in the first place.

🐾 Poems by db

🍀 Poems by rg

Indigo Dreams Publishing Ltd
24, Forest Houses
Cookworthy Moor
Halwill
Beaworthy
Devon
EX21 5UU
www.indigodreams.co.uk